Anthony KaDarrell Thigpen

IMPR**O**VE

Successful Strategies to Strengthen Self-Esteem

General Disclaimer

IMPROVE

Anthony KaDarrell Thigpen

Library of Congress Cataloging-in-Publication Data

Anthony KaDarrell Thigpen
Literacy in Motion Publications
Edited by Charmella Greer

IMPROVE
Successful Strategies to Strengthen Self-Esteem
ISBN: 978-0-692-99999-8

1. Self-help
Printed in the United States of America

Published by
Literacy in Motion, LLC
anthonykadarrellthigpen@gmail.com

IMPROVE

Successful Strategies to Strengthen Self-Esteem

Written by Journalist, Anthony KaDarrell Thigpen
Former Chicago Sun-Times/Post-Tribune News Correspondent

DEDICATION

If you've ever failed at anything, been disappointed by anyone, or felt rejected at anytime, this book is written in honor of you. It is dedicated to people who desire self-improvement in every aspect of life.

CONTENT

VIII

Introduction

AND IT BEGINS
How Insecurities Are Born

Let me start by saying I am not a psychologist, therapist or licensed counselor. By sharing my personal vulnerabilities, I'm able to help others climb out of life's darkest pitfalls. Everyday, I consciously aim to be a better me. Aiming to improve life demands discipline and time. I realize that the people who need to read this book the most, usually lack self-control and opportunity. Hopefully this book will captivate your attention and inspire you to improve your life. Everybody has room for improvement – nobody's perfect. It's important to create realistic goals and make time each day to create the kind of disciplines needed to improve your life. I've achieved some major life accomplishments as published on AnthonyThigpen.com, but I'm still making progress one day at a time. Nothing worthwhile comes easy or free – life is not a lottery. I've had a difficult road to travel, with potholes, detours, and delays. I've failed miserably, shamefully, and repeatedly. Failure is like checkpoints on the roadmap to happiness, success, and fulfillment. You have to take risks. I've been down so many dead ends roads with high hopes only to experience the sensation of feeling lost. I've had to turn around and try again far more times than I can count. This book paints portraits of difficult experiences with hopes to inspire readers to stay the course.

Improve is an anthology of personal testimonies mixed with accounts of anonymous characters as seen from my perspective. As an objective and experienced journalist, I'm trained to dig deep, ask difficult and necessary questions, and believe that everybody has a story worth sharing. Everyday, I hear another triumphant tale, while continuing to keep my fingers on the pulse of brokenhearted individuals. I've been blessed with an undying interest in helping hurting people do more than merely survive – I want to see survivors soaring. So many people are carrying the baggage of painful events that happened years ago, even decades. I know this all too well, because I used to do the same thing. Life does not come with an instruction manual. As a result, we all make miserable and shameful mistakes, and if you think you haven't, just keep living. Some people's worst mistake is thinking that their mistakes aren't as bad as other people's failures. There are also those who audibly admit that they are not perfect, but fail to embrace their specific imperfections in order to improve.

The most difficult obstacle is maneuvering around uncontrollable events, especially circumstances surrounding dysfunctional child-hoods, failed marriages, absent parents, war, rape, molestation and/or addictions. This next sentence could go in so many different directions at the crossroads of this book – the goal is to take the high road. There are so many amazing people who don't know how awesome they are. I've seen individuals smiling on the outside and damaged internally. I've been there too. As a result, this book is comprised of 5 chapters compacted into 90 pages of unintimidating easy-to-read strategies arranged to keep readers focused and positive. In effort to help readers maneuver over emotional mountaintops, I use my own compass. Growing up without my biological father created emotional insecurities. Fighting on the frontlines of the Iraq War created occupational insecurities. Battling issues of racial discrimination created social insecurities. These challenges have empowered me to give guidance to others during difficulties and crisis.

Perhaps your insecurities were born because you were molested, manipulated, raped, abused, impoverished, rejected, controlled, bullied, or even unwanted. The beginning of our frailties and vulnerabilities are usually centered on the same kryptonite that weakens us all – insecurities that damage our seven dimensions of wellness.

Of course most people publically deny vulnerability – being vulnerable is uncomfortable to say the least. Very few individuals freely dialog about their inferiorities and inadequacies. Instead, most people wear some type of mask – it's normal – you are not alone. This is why the chapter titles of this book are written in simple format, because most people are (chapter 1) ***Screaming Silently,*** *(chapter 2)* ***Living the Masquerade,*** *(chapter 3)* ***Failing to Embrace the Uneasy Truth,*** (chapter 4) ***Learning to Love Yourself First,*** and (chapter 5) ***Understanding What Matters in the End.*** These five short self-help chapters are the prescriptions I've use to overcome every past and present idea that victimizes my life to the point of insecurities.

Unquestionably, I admit I've needed some professional counseling to help navigate through rocky crossroads of my life. Unfortunately, as an African-American growing up in an urban setting, mental health challenges are often ridiculed as taboo. Black people are especially notorious at avoiding being labeled "crazy". Sadly, we also avoid getting the necessary help that will enable us to live functional and healthy lives. This reality is a damaging dynamics to the cultural climate of Black communities throughout the country. Regardless of the damage we endure, despite how broken we may be, we lean on other broken individuals. In the end, we prove again and again, that hurt people hurt people – misery loves company.

After fighting on the frontlines of the Gulf War, I did things to serve and defend my country that didn't leave me feeling proud. That's probably the best way to describe this seldom-disclosed chapter of my life. My dreams won't allow me to forget our unit motto, "One Shot, One Kill", and "Kill, kill, kill without mercy". I've tried to eradicate my mind from every battlefield memory, but my subconscious thoughts creep and crawl relentlessly. Every grueling memory and unreconciled thought, despite how desperately I dig to bury them alive, rise from the dead. For obvious reasons, I've tried to move pass that season of my life. I've pretended like killing didn't matter. I've questioned my own sanity every time I gained a sense of comfort or acceptance for having taken someone else's life. I've verbally blamed the government for sending such young soldiers on combat missions, but deep within I blamed myself. I've needed help. Even worse, the Department of Veteran Affairs juggled me through a system that made me realize that mental health professionals don't always have the answers. I kept seeking help. Eventually, I met a therapist that gave me a compass and the courage to face my biggest enemy – the man in the mirror. This battle could only be won by me. The most difficult battle of my combat experiences was fought in a dimly lit office while sitting on a sofa. During this season of my life, I realized that war was only another layer of scabs that formed on top of unresolved childhood wounds.

Truth is, I grew up with no knowledge of my biological father. I didn't even know his name. I'd always hoped that he'd come around and afford me the opportunity to feel normal. Well, at least back then I thought all the kids with dads felt like typical children. Probably sounds like no big deal in today's society, where more than 60-percent of children grow up in single-parent homes. It wasn't until I reached my mid-20's that I realized so many other people shared similar sentiments about their absent dads. There was always this tormenting thought about his identity. What does he look like? Why didn't he reach out to me? We often asked the same one-sided unanswered questions that lead us to the same dead end. These are not questions innocent children should have to ask themselves. We all experience feelings of rejection, resentment, and anger. This is how our greatest insecurities were born.

In retrospect some of my challenges weren't as complicated as they seemed in the heat of the moment. Difficult circumstances get exaggerated when feelings are unmanaged and weighed down with immaturity. I had no emotional security or direction in this area of my life. I wandered aimlessly with questions that went ignored. A man I never knew, who was supposed to love me, managed to mangle my mind with mixed emotions in his absence. Even worse, I wished death on my deadbeat dad. I hated him for being alive and making me live life as though he was dead. So many people are still wrestling with the same sense of rejection and lost identity. As a result, we grow up laughing, loving, and living like ordinary children, but inwardly, we carry the weight of warriors on the battlefield of life.

We wrestle deep within our subconscious. We wear the mask and pretend like dads don't matter. Simultaneously, we fail to effectively process and manage our anger. As a result, this pain spreads like a poisonous virus to every dimension of our lives. We fail to extinguish the wildfires of resentment that leave us feeling bitter about important areas of life. The experience of being rejected in younger years leave us feeling socially isolated. Ultimately, many of us jump through hoops seeking social acceptance as adults. Afterward, these feelings grow and shape our lives layer-by-layer, unless we tame the mixed-emotions that chokehold us into feeling like we have something to prove.

Reading *Improve* will help struggling children, empower hurting adults, and shed light on hidden wounds that are hindering relationships. This book will help people deal with difficulties of their past. My words are written to comfort and inspire people who have given up on the possibility of healing the scars that have gone untreated. Each chapter will intimately link with the hearts of readers and embody a hand-in-hand experience as we take a journey to complete wellness.

People who pretend like post-traumatic episodes of the past do not affect their present life, are only fooling themselves. I was one of those people for years. When I opened my eyes, removed my mask, and shed light beneath the layers of uncontrollable and unwanted circumstances and failures, my heart started healing.

I have finally reached a destination in life where it's okay to love each layered piece of my existence – failures and flaws included. This part of my journey wasn't easy, specifically because I couldn't do it alone. Honestly, when I returned from the war, I also contemplated suicide. Had a known how amazing my life would be those thoughts would have faded fast. Unfortunately, when we are sad, broken, feeling trapped, depressed and hurting, it's practically impossible to see the light at the end of our tunnel of tears.

On the outside, I've always worn a disposable mask etched with the description of a smiling face. Even now, a bright smile is my go-to expression. Inwardly, I didn't believe I would ever truly be happy. I'm almost ashamed to confess how miserable I was in life as a young adult. Like my childhood friend, Ryan, who I will discuss later, nobody knew how unhappy I felt day-to-day. My life didn't seem to make sense. Initially, I had no answers when I ran away from my childhood. Afterward, I ended up on the battlefield in Iraq. Pain propelled me from one lost season of life to the next. After wandering aimlessly for more than 40-years, I finally learned to love myself.

Details are so complicated that sometimes they have the potential to sound like excuses, and I despise excuses. So, I'll spare all pity parties. Our society simply has a problem trying to prove ourselves.

I'll be the first to plead guilty of this charge. Having something to prove once defined my spirituality, choice of college, physical physique, means of transportation, social circles and more. The only reason I'm not ashamed to admit it now is because I no longer have anything to prove to others. Initially, I'd titled this book, "Nothing to Prove". As I continued writing, I realized the more we embrace the reality that we have nothing to prove, the more our lives improve. As a result, I changed the title to this more inspirational expression of *Improve.*

Once we climb out the dark places of our consciousness, it's easy to pretend like we've never been there. Instead, reach back and help others escape. Far too many people have the audacity to pretend like they are better than their own past. This book will remind you that you are an improved culmination of all your past experiences.

I've felt so inadequate during some of the stormiest seasons of my life that I gave up and nobody even knew it. This is how my insecurities festered like open sores. The reason I'm writing *Improve* is to encourage others. I hope my vulnerable words burst into a brilliant awe-inspiring light for readers who genuinely want to improve.

The beginning of this journey is often the most difficult part. People seldom volunteer to conquer the demons that imprison their past. However, embracing your experiences will enrich your life more than you can envision. You're not required to write a book about your private experience, testify, or prove yourself to anybody. However, highlight passages of this book that impact you most. Start a private journal. Take notes always remembering that we are in this together. Making a commitment to start this personal journey to total wellness will serve as one of the most therapeutic and introspective experiences of your life.

Chapter **1**

SCREAMING SILENTLY

The Case against Suicide

My childhood friend committed suicide and nobody knows why. I used to feel guilty. I felt confused and hurt. We failed to stay connected when my family relocated. I didn't do anything to cause it, but I felt responsible having failed to listen or read between the lines. Perhaps I could have stopped it. I was only a child myself. As an adult, I've learned that people want to be accepted without judgment, and be treated with dignity. Carrying the weight of social rejection is extremely difficult for many people. I'm not sure why Ryan committed suicide. Others have done so because of depression, psychosis, impulse, attention, pain, and mistakes. People are naturally different, some cope with life's stresses, others succumb to the pressure. The heaviness of peer pressure, the death of loved-ones, broken families, rape, abuse, disease, alcoholism and various dysfunctions can result in poor mental health. Suicide victims don't all fit into cookie cutter scenarios that come with one quick fix.

This book is not an advocacy tool for suicide awareness. However, this chapter is chronologically scripted to first reach people who desperately need to improve their lives instead of ending it. The people you least expect are often the ones who commit suicide.

Even if a person is attractive, stylish, athletic, and has multiple friends, doesn't mean they aren't screaming for help on the inside. Everybody deserves to be heard, accepted and understood. Also, individuals must visualize a brighter future, embrace hopefulness, and see light at the end of every teary-eyed tunnel. Everybody needs to know there's a way of escape out of any dark situation. Unfortunately, this cruel modern world we live in isn't fair. In order for life to improve, we must accept the reality that we have nothing to prove. Had life's experiences etched this concept into the consciousness of my friend, perhaps he'd be alive to tell his story.

While growing up in a the Midwest in the 1970s, we played bitty basketball, little league baseball, kickball, hide-and-go-seek, and other made-up hands-on competitive sports like racing barefoot in the street. We also played board games like Monopoly, Trouble, and Connect Four. Girls jumped double-dutch and practiced cheerleading on the sidewalk, sometimes we all danced in the street listening to cassette tapes in boom boxes. We weren't poor, but the good ole days definitely included government issued cheese, which made the best grill cheese sandwiches. Our parents worked hard. We played outdoors. It seems like the entire community went to Sunday church services. There were no cellular devices, primarily rotary phones (we used our index finger to dial each number in a circular motion). Adults in the neighborhood had permission to discipline any child who lived nearby. Walking across the neighbors front lawn was unacceptable and a punishable offense. Our parents used tree branches and leather belts to "spank" us. There was no such thing as a "time out" for discipline. Our huge floor model box-shaped televisions had bunny rabbit antennas wrapped with alumni foil for better reception. We used dictionaries and type-writers, because computers didn't exist. Girls and boys wore wide leg bell bottom pants. French braids were popular. During those days African Americans sought to affirm our cultural identity by not straightening or cutting our hair. Boys used afro picks designed with Black power fists on the end. We used to go roller skating nearly every weekend at a place called "Screaming Wheels". We never heard terms like gluten-free, dairy-free, and GMO-free. Musical lyrics had an inspirational message that seldom, if ever, included profanity. With television networks like BET and MTV, Soul Train sitcoms highlighted R&B music as the soundtrack to our lives.

Along with his teacher Socrates, and his most famous student, Aristotle, the classical Greek philosopher Plato, laid the foundations of Western philosophy and science. Concerning music Plato wrote, "Forms and rhythms in music are never altered without producing changes in the entire fabric of society". Plato could not have been more on point. He was keenly aware. When the music changed, so did our culture. Music is an art form, and entertainers need to recognize its influence. Since 1946, we've transitioned from the "Baby Boomers" born from 1946 - 1964, to "Generation X" born from 1965 to 1976. Afterward, we watched the cultural impact of "Millennials" born from 1977 to 1995, to "Generation Z" born from 1996 to present. During each generational transition, the music has changed, and as a direct result, so did our culture, for the good and bad.

Wholesome living was the landscape of my childhood. Since then, suicide rates have increased tremendously. According to the American Foundation for Suicide, over 30,000 people in the United States die by suicide every year. For ages 15-24, suicide is the third leading cause of death. Every 16 minutes, a person dies from suicide in America. So, every day, approximately 80 Americans take their own lives, and 1,500 more make an attempt. Suicide is a silent way of saying goodbye to the pain that so many victims aren't able to cope with. When people are happy, hopeful, and feel like their life is improving, suicide is not an issue. The more culture changes, with aggressive music lyrics, cyberbullying, and drug misuse, suicide rates rise. We are now living in a culture driven by selfishness, selfies, and social media. Narcissism is the new narrative and backdrop of today's society. "Me, me, me," self-love, self-admiration, selfies and self-absorption is an epidemic counteracting wholesome living.

Suicide is the result of emotional emptiness, hopelessness and darkness. In a world with 7 billion human beings, countless people feel alone and lonely. Feelings like loneliness and boredom derive from idle thinking during seasons of clinical and circumstantial depression. Clinical depression warrants a diagnosis and treatment from a licensed professional. Circumstantial depression is derived from difficult life events that time usually heals. What's actually sad is that people hold others accountable for their well being. Wholeness is when you are not dependent on anyone or anything to supply you with a sense of joy. While positive people have a tendency to spread glad tidings, it is a risky reality to depend on others for your happiness. It's nobody's responsibility to make you happy, even if they previously have. You have to take the difficult steps to consciously improve your life. Far too many people are blaming others for their misery and unhappiness. This is the epitome of a pity party saturated with excuse and blame. Two things to remember when you experience such episodes. First, if you are the person being targeted, do not accept the blame, do not allow yourself to be manipulated, and do not plead guilty. Secondly, if you are unhappy, nothing will change until you take action, learn how to love yourself, and stop meditating on the rhetorical and emotional mess in your life.

Don't think that others are responsible to fix your brokenness. Communicate when you have an issue, as opposed to displaying the nonverbal attitude of an immature child. Stop trying to change others and change yourself, especially if you own the problem. Nobody wants to share your misery. However, my heart shatters into pieces watching tears fall, and listening to heart-broken individuals say, "I'm just tired". These three words echo as verbal distress signals – Save Our Souls (S.O.S.). I will probably never know why my friend Ryan committed suicide. What I do know is that people who feel like they need help don't always know how to communicate the way they feel. Articulating feelings and emotions can be quite difficult, until you routinely put forward the effort to establish the habit of doing so. On the other hand, caring people understand the importance of paying close attention to loved ones. Listen to what they have to say, without enabling them or feeding into their situation. Be very careful when you give people opinionated advice about their relationships. Give people your undivided attention when they are talking to you, and expect the same. Passively asking via impersonal text messages, "How are you" is not enough to reach the human hearts of hurting souls. We have to put away our electronic devices, focus on relationships that matter, and prioritize people with eye contact and engaged conversation.

Again, I'm no therapist. Since the loss of my childhood friend, I've taken this matter very personally and seriously. Ryan's loss will be the last personal experience of suicide in my life. So far, I'm proud to say, I've talked many people off the ledge, so to speak. I've sat in psychiatric wards supporting friends. I've gotten out of bed in the middle of the night to redirect fatal decisions. More than anything, I've learned that you can help people step-by-step to encourage suicide prevention. Having a sense of sincerity and a caring heart is something that needs to come natural.

10 Strategies to Help Someone Who is Contemplating Suicide

1. Start by asking, **"Have you felt this way before"?** This will enable you to understand whether the person you're trying to help suffers from clinical or circumstantial depression.

2. **Genuinely care about people** – enough for it to show authentically. This is crucial because an individual threatening suicide already feels hopeless, lonely and like no one cares.

3. **Make objective encouraging compliments** that will engage individuals into dialoging about their own quality characteristics.

4. **Do not be afraid to talk about suicide**, and be the person to walk him or her through the process of getting professional help.

5. **Be non-judgmental and non-accusatory while listening** with an open mind. Do not argue with them or try to convince them that their situation isn't that bad.

6. **Speak clearly, directly and be candid.** Don't beat around the bush, ask what you need to know and say what you need to say – be persistent.

7. **Know your audience.** Silence can feel somewhat uncomfortable for some and necessary for others. Remember, most suicide victims are screaming silently, and it's your job to allow their pain to speak to your heart.

8. **Let them speak.** Do not, under any circumstances, interrupt what a person is saying with threatening suicide. You never want a suicide victim to feel like you're calling them a bluff.

9. **Express gratitude for their trust.** Repeatedly thank them for being open and honest with you.

10. **Come up with an optimistic plan** and make a deal with the person to follow through with it.

I have an amazing network of close family and friends. My greatest asset gained from these relationships is always knowing that I have nothing to prove. As a result, I seldom feel misjudged, falsely accused, nor lonely. Obviously, misunderstandings occur in life. However, when I learned the value of my family members and friendships, my life improved. Also, the more I rid my life of the snakes, bloodsuckers, and chameleons that manipulate their way into our circles, improvement radically escalates. I still treat these individuals with dignity, but I do so from a distance.

Individuals who are not practicing law in a court room, gain no reward devaluing their time trying to prove themselves to others. It does not matter what role a person plays in your life, always keep reminding yourself that you have nothing to prove. Surrounding yourself with the right people is empowering. Positive people will effortlessly impart a vortex of tranquility. They will indirectly and non-aggressively impact your life with positivity. Avoid individuals that are two-faced. Avoid negative individuals who seldom have positive things to say. Avoid naysayers. Avoid individuals who are critics that disguise disapproval as constructive criticism. Avoid individuals who fail to make you feel good about yourself. Avoid individuals who are in denial about being miserable in their own lives. If you choose not to avoid these individuals, do so at your own risk, and rest assured that you will pay a price.

I could practically guess what readers might be thinking. How do you avoid individuals who live with you? How do you avoid individuals you're co-parenting with? How do you avoid parents, siblings, and spouses, without negativity? You know where I'm going with this, and I know what your dilemma is. This is not necessarily an easy task for most. Although, in order to permanently occupy your happy place, you've got to triumph over the obstacle of negative people, no matter who they are or what title they hold.

I realize I'm different from most. I'll disconnect, delete, and deny the very existence of anyone who tries to break me down. Whether they're using lies, rumors or truth to harm, they all fit in the same category. Here's what I learned over the years, I quickly forgive, let it go, and move on. However, I am always prepared to disconnect and distance myself for a season. Ignoring your perpetrator is not a bad thing to do, as long as you are not avoiding the idea of dealing with your own self-created-chaos. As a result, my stern and steadfast approach usually prompts misguided loved-ones to apologize and change their ways. Sometimes, I have to do the same – I am not always in the right. However, tolerating people who don't promote and publicize what's best for you is a dangerous trap. I commonly practice my self-invented "7 Billion Rule". There are more than 7 billion people on this planet, and while I value every individual as a positive fixture in my life. At the end of day, there are far too many human beings on the planet to allow a few negative naysayers to drag me through dark and dirty gutters.

There's a sense of emotional security we get from connecting with people that don't make us feel like we have anything to prove. Once we secure this kind of relationship, life starts immediately improving. As long as you allow emotional and social parasites to drain you, your life will not reach its maximum potential.

Most miserable people simply don't have a comprehensive roadmap to escape their dismal life of defeat. Individuals who screw-up their lives seem to secretly want others to come under their umbrella. These people are so busy trying not to get caught in the rain again, that they try to block others from living their lives. People have to make their own decisions, even if that leaves them singing in the rain. For example, envision the single mother who has no respect for abstinence until marriage; or the terminated worker who wants existing employees to have a negative view of the company; or the divorcee who has a pessimistic view of marriage. Others hate to see your life blossoming before theirs. Jealously is cruel and vicious. There are also people that are intimidated by the possibly of you doing better than they are with personal achievements. I could on, but I think my point is clear – everybody is not a good ingredient for the recipe of your success.

Now, that doesn't mean that they don't deserve to be treated with dignity, but you can do that from a distance. You don't have to argue with anyone – quarreling adds no value – it will drain you and leave you ineffective. You don't have to debate your position. You have nothing to prove. This is your life. Isn't it interesting that people who have made their own mistakes and poor choices somehow manage to have all the perfect answers for your life? I choose to glean from success, not the failures of naysayers. Remember, it's not your responsibility to get them to see your point of view. Let it go. You don't need a meeting, a counseling sessions, one last phone call, or another text message. Just let it go. Once your life improves, perhaps they'll be ready for the new and improved you, but you have to realize that you have nothing to prove to others. Most likely you've already heard the expression, "Hurt people hurt people". Break the cycle by removing yourself from the drama-filled episodes that causes you to miss countless opportunities. Television provides me with all the drama I'm willing to entertain.

Recently, I asked my 11-year-old daughter a series of questions. As a dad, I needed to know how she felt about her self-image. I asked about her self-esteem. I asked her to tell me how she envisioned her future. I even asked about her relationships at school, from friends to bullies. As awkward as it might sound, I went as far as to ask her how she feels about being a Black student at a predominantly White school. It's important for me to know that I'm imparting emotional strength, personal confidence, and a strong sense of self-esteem. In this cruel culture created by a society of profane music, bullies, and hurt people, I'm determined to be the guardian over her healthy development. This is how I initiate the best case against suicide. I shed light on the darkness that tries to cast unwanted shadows in any area of her life. Upon thoroughly questioning her, visiting her classroom, chaperoning field trips, volunteering during three-day camping trips, interacting with her daily, and talking with her teachers and peers, I concluded that my daughter is developing wonderfully.

I also wear a lot of professional hats, from journalist, publisher and philanthropist, to videographer and photographer. As a professional photographer, one of my responsibilities include being conscious of shadows. Sometimes, shadows are useful, but unwanted shadows will ruin an otherwise great photo. My goal in this chapter is to capture a strong and solid case against suicide. *Improve* aims to snap the kind of images that will empower people to feel good about themselves, flaws included. Instead of allowing people to suffer and scream silently, this book speaks to the heart to heal hurting people. We all know that one picture can speak a thousand words. When we listen to individuals that is screaming silently, we can shed light simply by embodying their experience.

If you are emotionally distressed, or in a suicidal crisis, or know someone who might be, please get help. Even if you are a military veteran who needs help coping, contact the **National Suicide Prevention Lifeline at 1-800-273-8255.** You deserve to be heard. Stop screaming silently, and reposition your life to improve.

This chapter is written in memory of my childhood friend, Ryan Beverly – I will always remember him. So many people, young and old, from pastors to fathers, are alive because of how his death impacted my life. My thoughts of "Ry" have caused me to help so many hurting people – to include myself, during the worse episode of my life. I've etched your name in this book with the hopes that your short life will never be forgotten.

Chapter **2**

LIVING THE MASQUERADE

Faults, Failures and Fears

Believe in yourself. Don't get so caught up in the career goal or personal ambition you want to accomplish, be true to your present day self. Otherwise you'll get lost in your imagination. You have to also believe in the process. Don't hide and mask your true identity – eventually a piece of your greatness will start withering. Afterward, you won't even recognize the real you. So many people are trying to "keep up with the Joneses'". It's common in our society for individuals to mask their faults, failures and fears. As a result, some of the most "would be" amazing personalities are living the masquerade. Faults, failures and fears are designed to test our character and make us better, not to embarrass us. Live your life shame-free and regret-free. That doesn't mean you shouldn't apologize for wrongdoings or feel bad for hurting others. Neither does it mean you have to advertise your weaknesses to the world. Living a shame-free and regret-free life merely means that you must allow yourself room to grow – growth brings about failures and challenges.

As a baby, like most infants, my daughter started crawling. Afterward, she started taking tiny steps. She fell so many times, but she always got back up. Now she's running and jumping. Recently, she learned to swim and roller skate. Initially, the learning curb made her feel like a failure, but she kept trying until one day she discovered herself swimming the full length of the pool, and skating like a champ. We all fail, fall, and falter in life - it's how we get stronger, better, and wiser. Life is a culmination of both desirable victories and unwanted experiences. Most importantly, get comfortable in your own skin - be confident - and remember to always believe in yourself.

This strategy will cause your life to improve so rapidly that you'll see your own mirror image changing. I used to be more than 90 pounds heavier in 2017. I'm not sure which image I hated worse, looking at the scale, or seeing myself in the mirror unclothe. It seems like I had every reason to lose weight, but every excuse not to. I'd exercise and then quit - eat healthy and then binge - accept being overweight, and then look in the mirror and feel miserable again. It was a vicious cycle. All the while, I kept smiling and pretending like I was happy. I certainly wasn't happy about my weight. I wasn't happy about being borderline obese. I wasn't happy about being prehypertension. I wasn't happy about fearing the onset of Type II Diabetes. But I kept wearing the mask, until I decided to be honest with myself.

With one sentence, a friend reminded me how healthy I used to be. "Bro, you've gained a lot of weight, you used to really be in shape," that's all he said. He didn't mean any harm. I knew that because even his reminiscent constructive criticism oozed with positivity. His words pierced me with deep conviction to live a consistently healthier lifestyle. Unlike virtual friendships digitally perpetuated on Instagram, Facebook, Snapchat and other forms of social media, true friendship inspires. His words were just enough to make me believe that if I did it before, I could do it again. I changed my diet. I committed to a vegan lifestyle. I stopped eating meat, poultry, seafood, or animal products like cheese, milk, sour cream and butter. Initially it was difficult. I didn't know what recipes to prepare. So, I started eating all sorts of beans, fruit, vegetables, nuts, wheat, and seeds. I thought to myself, if I fail, I'd wake up the next day and start again, but I didn't fail – not at this, anyway. Soon after, I started drinking lots of water, getting quality sleep, walking, and then running, and now I spend hours in the gym. Me, in the gym, almost sounds like an oxymoron. Seventy-pounds later and I needed a new wardrobe. I no longer have to pretend like I am happy with my weight. Sure, it's an ongoing struggle, but so was the unrewarding effort I put into living the masquerade. I found myself living an unhealthy lifestyle, pretending like it had no adverse effect, because wellness demands discipline.

When I deliberately stopped living the masquerade my life immediately improved. From extreme weight loss, increased credit score, new website (Anthony.Thigpen.com), new book release, and so much more. When you wear the mask, your real identity is isolated from improvement. Stop pretending. Stop being dishonest with yourself. You're only hindering your own self-improvement. The imagination is dangerous. It will have you painting phantom pictures and living an illusion. There is only one reality. This new-aged cultural concept that everybody has their own reality is a mentally unhealthy deception. The expression "Just do you" is ruthlessly counterproductive. By nature, it deteriorates social wellness. Nobody seeks to connect with, nor commit to individuals who only choose to evaluate life from their "reality". A "reality" is based on what is real. The definition of the word reality is "the state of things as they actually exist, as opposed to an idealistic or notional idea of them". Our new-aged society of self is saturated with individuals who are socially lazy. Generation X and Z make excuses to avoid effective and accountable communication. As a result, it is currently commonly said that everybody has their own reality. This poorly misguided philosophy is no way to enhance your life. It will validate and trap young people into hopeless situations and justify the masquerade lifestyle.

We all may have different opinions and perspectives about reality, despite how ambiguous, facts are actualities. You cannot improve your reality while living in a delusion. People will come at you with all sorts of opinionated negativity, if you allow it. Once you commit to getting an education, they'll say, "You think you're better than us". When you start paying off debt, they'll ask, "Can I borrow...". When you decide to get married, they'll plant a seed, "Are you absolutely sure she/he is the right one?"[2] Improving your life will take an intentional effort to hurdle over people who always seem to remind you of past faults, failures and fears. In the event that you've been damaged in your past, that doesn't mean you should avoid healthy risks and positive relationships in your future. Take responsibility of your failures and be a better judge of your outcomes. Don't crawl beneath a rock and let great opportunities pass you by because you didn't evaluate previous situations adequately.

My skin crawls at the thought of unproductive and unnecessary confrontation. Although I'm a great debater that communicates well, I still don't like wrestling with conflict – it causes unwarranted anxiety. This kind of stress is statistically proven to shorten human lifespan. So, before you engage in your next quarrel, conflict, or confrontation, ask yourself is it really worth shortening the days of your life. Obviously, this dilemma raises a red flag. Most of us have had to deal with an argumentative friend. When we share our lives with other people, whether spouse, family, friend, neighbor or co-worker, a level of responsibility and humility is required from both personalities. We are all far from perfect. Although that is no excuse to allow anyone to slowly smother your identity. Let's face it, some people don't like you the way you are, so they'll try to force you to be who they want you to be. Even worse, they'll throw jabs and darts and then deny their cruel intentions. Some of the most difficult people to deal with are "frienenemies", because they wear a mask in order to stay connected. "Frienenemies" are enemies disguised as friends. Whenever we try to convince ourselves that disingenuous relationships are acceptable, nothing improves. People who have pure intentions, positive motives, and kind hearts won't add unnecessary stress to your life. When confrontation is necessary amongst unpretentious friends, you don't have to hide behind a sword and shield in order to have a peaceful conversation. It's clear when people mean well.

"Frienenemies" prey on your failure, faults and fears. They want you to feel insecure, be a low achiever, and continue living the masquerade. These individuals are easy to recognize. They always talk about people, places and things. They gossip. They target negativity, and then aimlessly destroy. They lack discipline, and they wear one mask with you and another with others. On the other hand, true friendships are invaluable. Friends discuss goals, ideas, and ambitions. Friends freely share love, kindness, peace, patience, and characteristics that build, instead of tearing down. When you notice that you have a "frienenemy" masquerading in your circle, do not retaliate, confront, or declare war. Simply walk away, because you have nothing to prove. Spare yourself the stress – save yourself.

I get it. In theory, it's easy to say what you 'would do' or what somebody 'should do'. It takes a sense of courage to stand alone, walk alone, and be true to yourself, especially when you know your own flaws. What you must aim to avoid under any circumstances is pretending to be perfect. People often highlight the failures of others hoping to mask their flaws. Don't be a fraud. It's difficult embracing our failures, acknowledging our faults, and facing our fears. It's much easier to simply deny and dismiss all that is undesirable about ourselves. I think I understand why most people put on the public mask and live the masquerade. On a surface level, wearing masks make sense. Dealing with our own struggles, weaknesses, and challenges is a surmounting obstacle. As a result, it's easier to focus on the flaws and failures of others. Although, gossip does not birth greatness. It just makes miserable people feel a false sense of normalcy. However, I'd suggest that if you want to see some personal improvement in your life, be true to yourself.

Nobody's perfect. Stop measuring your faults, failures and fears against the spreadsheet of other people's lives. The social media portrayal of people is usually false and deceptive. People tilt their heads down and hold the camera phones high to alter images, because this makes overweight people look small. They post narratives that influence people to think their lives are fairytale stories. Most people share information and images on social media aiming to manipulate and control what viewers think. People make posts specifically to get likes and views from digital friends and fans. Social media is not a healthy platform for building self-esteem - it's quite the opposite. It will inflate you with flattery. Afterward, the more you engage and engulf your self-worth into the virtual reality of social media, the less meaningful your real life becomes. Social media is virtual reality. Social media is predominantly about personal agendas, selfies and selfishness. No posts are believable at face value, because nothing is researched or fact checked. No one holds any individual accountable for false information, images, and/or ideas on social media. The rules to the digital masquerade party are simple – snap, speak your mind, and post. It's easy to masquerade digital perfection on Facebook, Snapchat, and Instagram. However, life only improves when we face failures, faults, and fears – this is called facing reality.

Failure is not fatal. Failure can only lead to public shame when you care about what the public thinks. When you chisel the mantra into your consciousness that you have nothing to prove, you will attract improvement. Repeatedly and audibly say to yourself, "I have nothing to prove". Failure is the deepest pitfall we experience, because it causes delay, denial, defeat and depression. Instead of starting over, deal with reality. Most people just revert to the mask. The next time you fail, get back up, brush yourself off, and stay true to yourself.

Be careful not to brush off your failures and move on too quickly. At the same time, don't hold on to our failures so long that they turn into self-doubt and anxiety. Don't blame others and make excuses. Take ownership of your actions. This will empower you to redirect the course of your future. Also, don't deny your failures. Denying your failure impedes improvement. Lastly, don't give up so easily. Remember, we fail because it is part of our human experience. Failure doesn't minimize you as a person, it positions you for success. Yes, failure is necessary for victory.

Throughout my adulthood, I've personally and privately supported so many people during times of tragedy and loss. Whether through suicide attempts, cancer, HIV & AIDS, depression, abortions, and other indescribable experiences, I've learned to be an encouragement. I've watched individuals mask their pain, embarrassment, heartache, disappointment and shame with humor, deceit, and anger. I've cried with some, gotten aggressive with others, visited secured psychiatric facilities, sat silently in hospital rooms, and waited patiently in clinic parking lots. I pray and meditate. What many people value most is that I listened without judgment. Every individual I deal with realize there was no need for the masquerade. When you find a genuine friend that inspires you to disarm and let your guard down, cherish that kind of rare sanctity. I value the fact that people always seem to remove their mask with me – it means I'm doing something to make them comfortable. When people are treated with dignity the need for a mask no longer exist. I've learned to love beyond convenience and pass flattery without the need for eloquent speech. I intentionally show the kind of compassion that is unconditional. My compassion doesn't make me better than anyone else. It's just evidence that I need the same. Even when "frienenemies" betray me, their confidentiality remains safe in my care. The most valued treasures I'll take to my grave are the secrets shared by phenomenal people that trusted me during their most difficult days.

Most people I meet don't realize that I'm an introvert. Probably because I encounter a lot of people as a multimedia professional. As an introvert, I see people differently from most. During photo-shoots, clients commonly request post-editing of their images. I've been asked to digitally remove tattoos, moles, skin tags, double chins, shrink arms, delete acnes, lighten skin tones, and more. As an introverted photographer, I see these traits as unique textures when most people seem to despise their flaws. These attributes and beauty marks make us feel like we've failed to meet the mainstream standards of beauty. It makes us feel worthless, insignificant and weak. Fact is, removing the mask means embracing your identity, and getting comfortable in your own skin. When kindhearted individuals gain enough confidence to remove their mask, the world gets to see what true beauty looks like. Beauty is not some Hollywood portrayal of airbrushed makeup, liposuction, and/or silicone breast. Those are aspects that perpetuate the idea of living the masquerade. Your mistakes expose your humanity. Your failures cause you to be more compassionate, and your flaws are the beauty marks that make you unique. Believe in yourself enough to permanently remove the mask, expose your inner beauty, and watch the entire world improve around you.

Chapter **3**

FAILING TO EMBRACE THE UNEASY TRUTH

You Have Nothing to Prove to Others

Everybody wants happiness. The one word which contains the sole meaning of lifelong success. People achieve fame, gain financial prosperity and experience favor, but without happiness, nothing else matters. Without happiness life feels like an unoccupied corpse, cold and empty. Unhappy people always find themselves dissatisfied and yearning for more. I've learned a lot through my personal experiences. While traveling the world, meeting unique Americans and foreigners, I've seen happiness hide its face at times. Happiness is a fleeting idea when people live life trying to prove themselves to others. Once you realize that happiness has nothing to do with the "American Dream," your pursuit of happiness will gain a beneficial momentum.

Life is not a rat race. Neither is an accurate depiction of success an image of crabs in a bucket. Money and power does not equal success and happiness. My friends who live paycheck-to-paycheck chase money for happiness. My middle-class friends feel like they have something to prove in order to be happy. My financially wealthy friends feel emotionally challenged because of circumstances they cannot control. Happiness is a unique euphoric state-of-being that unequivocally makes people feel empowered about their own human dignity. When people experience this addictive sensation, whether rich or poor, sick or healthy, old or young, it will redefine any person's perspective of success. Truth be told, our end goal is not the house of the hill, proving yourself to others, nor being in control, it's living a happy life. This is why we work tirelessly at achieving the 7 dimensions of wellness. We graduate from school, work hard, seek promotions, change careers, get married, invest, have children, get divorced, retire, relocate, and more. These constant changes occur because every human being is yearning for a happy ending. We want wealth, purpose, and control, not just to say we have it, we think if we get it, it's going to make us happy. That is why life is truly all about the pursuit of happiness, because at the conclusion of each day, everybody is racing to the same thing, happiness.

Do all people deserve to be happy? Good question. People pursue plenty of things they don't deserve. We are notorious for perpetuating a self-serving society by constantly reaffirming things that are not deserved. My daughter once participated in a summer sports program. It struck me as odd that every child received a ribbon for racing whether they finished first or last. They're called participation ribbons. I'm not going to chime into this new-aged debate. However, we've got to be careful not to create a monstrous generation who rage around thinking they deserve something for nothing. Some people argue that, "It's not fair for only one child to get the trophy," (even though that hard working child happens to be the winner). Others agree, saying, "Trophies get kids motivated," (despite the opposite message sent to the kids which are already driven). The aged-old expression, "Hard work pays off," remains indisputable. This is why blanket (one-size-fits-all) compliments like "You deserve nothing but the best," and "You deserve to put yourself first," are counterproductive. If you get something that you didn't work for, that's called unmerited favor. Some might even say it borders favoritism – and this type of nepotism can be disabling. How about we start believing, "If you work for it, you deserve what comes". But competitively speaking, if someone worked harder than you, then it's likely that they'll prove more deserving. Don't feed into the counterproductive self-entitled mentality of thinking you deserve things that you didn't work to earn.

The very reason some people are not happy is because their thoughts are counter-productive. Would you work for a company knowing it's bankrupt and unable to pay its employees? I didn't (think) so. Why then do so many people put in the work amongst the wrong people, places and things? In the end, they're always even more miserable. This reminds me of the sweet-hearted college girl that only seems to be attracted to convicts, street thugs, and bad guys. Not that these individuals don't have dignity, their wayward misguided views cause them to be morally bankrupt. During and after the relationships, the tears and devastation of these girls reflect how they feel misused and violated. Once you've invested a piece of yourself into bankrupt individuals, there's no need to act perplexed when misused, railroaded and rejected. Common sense is not all that common in a society that encourages young people to do whatever floats their boat. When void of moral principles, individuals are destined to exercise a counterproductive philosophical approach.

Another example would be, employees complain about their jobs and do nothing to improve their occupational wellness. They invest in emotionally abusive relationships ignoring their own social wellness. They fail to recognize that their frustrations spiral from their own dysfunctional efforts of trying to control others. Many people can't depend on themselves for things they're responsible for, but these same people have high expectations of others. This frustration causes the lack emotional wellness. Some people seek happiness through manipulative strategies of perversion, con artistry, negative attitudes, and lies. We are all born with the innate desire to strive for happiness. This inescapable human passion is the driving force that causes individuals to act. Some of these actions are good and others are bad, but they all reflect the energy sacrificed for happiness. So, while we all deserve to be happy, happiness won't happen for many people. Counteractive actions of miserable, hurting, and conniving individuals will prevent them from ever experiencing the euphoric energy of true happiness.

Indeed, you deserve to be happy, and so does everyone else. Unfortunately, many have condemned themselves and ostracized others. Good thing is, in spite of the past, and despite what is happening currently, there remains a potential for happiness. This potential is manifested when good-hearted people are willing to exercise the right principles to achieve it. Happy people are in every walk of life. Some have made mistakes, like ex-convicts, murderers, deadbeat parents, rapists, and the like. Others have unattractive flaws, shameful failures, and unspoken fears. Happiness does not discriminate. Only unhappy individuals think they have the right to decide who should and should not be happy.

Even if someone hurts you deeply, perhaps they murdered your dearest loved one, happiness still will not forfeit their future. Happiness will however disappear from your life, as long as you are focused on seeking revenge on others. When people are judgmental and unforgiving, it's very likely that they are unhappy. In most cases, they are secretly miserable. By nature, revenge is spiteful – and it does not leave room for justice. Happiness is impartial to wrongdoings. Like most, I've endured some deep seated betrayal, lies, and mistreatment, but I've learned that forgiveness is powerful. And my forgiving heart attracts happiness.

Unfortunately, there are those who have every material possession desired, but remain unhappy. Happiness is not materialistic, physical, or subjective. Sometimes known illnesses and undiagnosed mental conditions are huge obstacles for emotionally struggling people. However, happiness is like an irreplaceable friend who shares friendship with your enemies. I'm trying to describe that friend who always wants to keep the peace. That friend who refuses to hear negative opinions about either side. That friend whose loyalty is questioned because he/she won't take sides under any circumstances. Our response to those kind of friends is exactly how we respond to happiness. We devalue it. We question it. We try to control it. This is why some people will die unhappy, because they've never been taught how to value happiness.

There is a huge difference between what makes people feel good as opposed to happiness. People, places, and things have the ability to make you feel good, but they can also make you feel bad. A perfect example of a place that makes people feel good and then feel bad are casinos – winning and losing has that effect. Could you possibly conceive the idea of happiness making someone unhappy? Of course not. It wouldn't be sane to say, "I'm so happy that I'm unhappy". Happiness will never make you unhappy. Furthermore, an individual can embrace you, and then betray you. A place like a casino can appeal to you, and then make you feel miserable. Certain things like medicines can help you, but also harm you with side effects. But happiness has one goal, and that is for you to be happy. It is just that simple. Remember, happiness is a unique euphoric state-of-being that makes people feel empowered by their own human dignity. When you feel a positive sense of euphoric empowerment, your life will inevitably improve. Illegal drug users, alcohol abusers, sexual deviants, excessive eaters, and similar addictive behaviors diminish with happiness.

Happiness protects people from self-depravations. When people are miserably searching for happiness in the wrong places, we often change for the worse. We find ourselves deteriorating into a downward spiral of morbid perversions when we confuse happiness with sensations that make us feel good. There is a distinct difference between feeling good and being happy.

Unhappiness is a blinding poison that will rob you from your true identity, self-worth, and hope. Society warns of suicidal scenarios, but rarely explain how unhappiness will decay, deteriorate, and destroy human lives. "Morbid perversion" is a phrase used by physician James Cowles Prichard, who first described morale insanity in 1835. He defined it as, "madness consisting in a morbid perversion of the natural feelings, affections, inclinations, temper, habits, moral dispositions, and natural impulses, without any remarkable disorder, defect of interests, nor reasoning faculties, and particularly without any insane illusion or hallucinations."

In essence, when people are unhappy they do immoral and insane activities without actually realizing why. They do discouraging things that make them feel worse. These actions do not merely make people feel physically worse because of hangovers, diseases, financial losses, unwanted pregnancies and more. It also further diminishes their self-worth, moral discretion, and overall view of life. Happiness is invaluable. It opens our eyes to a world of positivity. Our greatest asset is not health or wealth, it's happiness.

Instead of always asking people "What should I do" and then doing nothing, happiness requires an action. People seek advice and do nothing afterward. These meaningless conversations fail to motivate individuals to act. Each dimension of wellness requires action on your part. If you ever expect to improve your overall state of wellness, you've got to be willing to "put your money where your mouth is". Don't merely admit your weaknesses, take the next step and do something about them. An unknown author once said, "The definition of insanity is repeatedly doing the same thing and expecting a different result". If this is you, it's never too late to start engaging solutions to secure your happiness.

Chapter **4**

LEARNING TO LOVE YOURSELF FIRST

Be Your Own Best friend

It's difficult to balance the art of living life selflessly while trying to love yourself first. One of the easiest ways this is ever going to happen is to see your happiness as an individual asset. Once you acknowledge happiness as your most priceless asset, you'll start seeing yourself differently. You will guard your heart from anybody and anything that puts your happiness in jeopardy. I used to be so concerned about standing up for the underdog; feeding the homeless, mentoring the fatherless, and speaking up for the voiceless. The more I focused on others, the less I had time to love myself. I still care about the good of all humanity, but I've learned to balance my charitable passions with my personal well being.

Years ago, I used to actually argue that selfless people couldn't possibly love themselves. It seemed like a rhetorical contradiction to me. I've always been taught the perspective of putting others before myself. This concept went as far as to express the importance of "giving others the shirt off my back" if necessary. I know now this concept contradicts the first law nature and self-preservation. Truth is, when you best take care of yourself, then you can adequately take care of others. When you make the decision to unconditionally treat yourself with dignity, then you'll know how to treat others. We cannot effectively love others until we've learned to love ourselves. I can't help supply other people's needs if I don't supply my own. Some people use the self-preservation reality as an excuse for selfishness. Self-preservation has nothing to do with greed, luxury, and waste. Improving your life starts with loving yourself first, and then caring about all of humanity.

The expression 'love yourself first' has nothing to do with self-indulgence. When people are asked to define what love means, most replies start with an explanation based on feelings. It took me a lot of pain, time, and experience to learn that true love transcends feelings. More than anything, love is a decision. It's not a mistake that we "fall into" or something that just "ends up happening". Love is a conscious choice to be willingly vulnerable enough to expose your inner soul. It's a decision to invest introspectively into compassionately understanding a human life. Love is a sacrificial choice to commit to consistently changing in effort to enrich, empower, and embody enlightening experiences. As human beings, we cannot effectively experience this kind of love for others, unless we first love ourselves.

Starting with yourself first, **STEP 1.** Remove all the masks and stand face-to-face with the person in the mirror; take a raw, honest look at the person you've become. **STEP 2.** Examine your insecurities, struggles and flaws to understand your failures without blaming others. Evaluate successes without feeding your ego. Get to know yourself. (Question: should you explain what get to know yourself means? Just a thought.) **STEP 3.** Be willing to consistently change in order to improve, enable, and personify edifying experiences. Become the improved happy version of yourself that can interact with people without having anything to prove.

Unless you follow similar steps, the vicious cycle of unhappiness, misery and brokenness will continue to spiral. Get your life together. When you learn how to love yourself first, it's impossible for your life to lack improvement. These strategies produce guaranteed results. Taking the right steps to love yourself first is a fail-safe strategy for success.

I most warn you, following this strategy will cause some unexpected results. Let me caution you about a few surprise personalities you might meet along the way. People have preconceived and unspoken expectations about your life. Other people have scripts that they want you to stick to no matter what. Perhaps because it is natural to expect more of the same from individuals we interact with daily. People don't usually like change. Expectations give most insecure people a sense of security. When you make the decision to improve your life, these unspoken opinions and unread scripts often echo without reason. There are several types of friendships you should to be aware of.

First, I experienced **THE JEALOUS FRIEND.** In short, this is the friend who had a wife, three children, a beautiful 3-story home, a great career, and so much more. On the other hand, I was a bachelor, with no children, living in a two-bedroom apartment. After I purchased a home, got married, and had a beautiful daughter, I thought for sure our lives would share similar interests. Instead, after two-decades of friendship, he stopped talking to me. Years later, he explained the embarrassing difficulties that led to his divorce. He candidly told me that he was jealous because I was publicly experiencing the happiness he privately no longer had. Remember, the people who you'd expect to be happiest when your life improves might surprise you.

Such is the case with **THE JUDGMENTAL FRIEND**. This friend might seem like the greatest most accepting person in the world. Based on their own personal experiences shared, I thought nothing I could vent about could be poorly perceived. I suddenly found myself listening to someone trying to influence me leave my faithful wife, who was still married despite infidelity. Even worst, our irreconcilable friendship boiled down to my failure to bow down to opinions about my marriage. When their marriage was broken, I repeatedly helped. When mine went through challenges, they aimed to destroy. When I rejected their judgment, they became a "frienenemy". Take this as a word of advice, people don't regard their own miserable situations as pathetically as they try to paint a picture of yours.

Next would be **THE SELFISH FRIEND.** They're quite annoying because most selfish people are so into self that they don't recognize it. No matter what I've discovered about myself along this introspective journey, this friend makes everything himself. He knows everything. He's experienced everything, and of course always before me. His solutions are the only proper approach to problem solving, investing, and relationships. His personal life didn't go as planned, so he lives vicariously through mine. In his view of things, his decisions about my life are more important than my own. While there is greatness in this friendship, he's difficult to be around at times, especially when you're trying to celebrate your victories. He will drain you if you allow it, financially, emotionally, and socially. Unfortunately, he has a lot to say about what I should do differently. Yet, he is suddenly silent when it's time to celebrate my successes. Beware of selfish people.

Now, of course, I've encountered other types of friends, too. **The flaky friend, the negative friend, and the friend who encourages bad choices.** Even worse is **the user friend, the fat-shaming friend, the friend who dogs you out behind your back.** I made a decision along life's journey to be my own best friend. I decided to encourage myself, give myself constructive criticism, celebrate my successes, and examine my failures. I still have other friendships, even childhood friends. I have veteran friends, neighborhood friends, religious friends, and working friendships I've established throughout my career. I have several remarkable friends I could boast about, but my most esteemed example of friendship is with a California native named Ernest.

We've been like brothers for an uninterrupted period of 25 years. We've stood the test of time. We've stood as best men in one another's weddings. I flew in town and stood bedside in the hospital supporting his heart transplant. He flew in town and stood nearby during my first book signing. We built our brotherhood when telephone carriers charged per minute for long distance calls. Before the advancement of email, cellular devices, and personal laptops, we wrote one another letters regularly. Years of shared effort went into our brotherhood. Finances, opinions, nor attitudes created adverse unwanted energy between us. Within 25 years, we've avoided arguments, despite differences. We've never judged each other, and we've always made one another feel safe enough to communicate life's most critical challenges. Our personalities are nothing alike, I'm welcoming, and he's not. I smile more often than not; he usually maintains a straight face. Over the years, his influence has taught me to guard my heart and mind. Many of my stern social stipulations are a direct result of his indirect influence. However, he doesn't voice any aggression to sway my opinions. He never attempts to control my actions, manipulate my thoughts, or misuse my talents and resources. As a result of his friendship, I've avoided countless heartache, unnecessary arguments, and distanced myself from many "frienenemies". The attributes I share with Ernest is a blueprint for what I expect in all my other unique friendships. People like Ernest have empowered me with a safe haven to live my life free of having anything to prove to people. It would be perfect if everybody could have at least one friendship like ours. Until yours come along, don't settle for less, and be your own best friend. Ultimately, true friendship is when you are safe enough to be vulnerable knowing that you can express what makes you feel free.

Freedom is born in the idea of learning to "love yourself first". When children are taught how to love themselves first, bullies have no effect. Young adults can avoid painstaking and sensation-driven relationships when they understand love. When you love yourself first, you set a standard of how others are expected to love and treat you. Embracing the idea of loving yourself first will impart two amazing characteristics in your life. First, it will heighten your compassion for others. If you don't "love yourself first" there's no assurance that you'll adequately love others. Secondly, loving yourself first will define borders for what you have a right to expect from others. There are countless spiritually misguided, secretly broken, silently hurting people looking for love. Unfortunately, hurt people hurt people. This relentless cycle will continue until people learn how to love themselves first. I'm grateful for the grace that allowed my marriage to survive for many years without this knowledge. If you take the letter "U" out of the alphabet, you lose 3000 words in our vocabulary. Sometimes it's the one thing we do wrong that takes the magic out of marriages and other relationships. After nearly 13 years, I'm now learning the missing words that possess the power to improve my most important relationship. The most critically challenging course of improving your life starts with liberating yourself from the pain caused by other people. Free yourself from everybody's rules and stipulations. This freedom is discovered when we love ourselves first.

Far too many people have double standards when it comes to relationships. Healthy relationships are created when we love and treat others like we want to be treated. As a child, my mother taught me this "Golden Rule" – it is priceless. There is a distinct difference between love vs. the temporary feel good sensation most people share early on in relationships. Individuals who define love based on feelings are at risk of being deeply hurt, devastated, and depressed. Feelings change. Love is steadfast. Feelings are difficult to control. As a result, some people feel like they are in love one day, and they'll claim to hate the same person the next. Love is a conscious decision. Based on our thoughts and admirations, despite suspicions and beliefs, love wins. Feelings and emotions always change. People can feel bad, sad, or lonely, and then happy, hopeful, or heroic, all in the same day.

Our actions and our attitudes are altered based on how we feel – feelings ignite energy and set certain behaviors in motion. This is why the word is called "E-Motions". It defines energy in motion. Love is more powerful than any feeling or emotion, but it also creates energy. Remember, unconditional love is a cognitive decision. It's not something that just happens without a measured standard.

People who do not have a standard suffer repeatedly from regret and disappointment. When you "love yourself first" the need for pity parties diminish. Far too many hurting people aim to dialog with others who have experienced similar devastation – no matter how you define it, that's called a pity party. They can relate. However, relating to other hurting people is not an effective strategy to improve your life. When the pity party ends, nothing changes. Group therapy and professional counseling is a different concept that does serve beneficial. Although, I've seen people relentlessly vent, say horrible things about an individual, express hate, and remain intimately interactive in the same unhealthy relationship. Pity parties stroke egos, bolster a false sense of connection between misguided individuals, and drums up rumors based on one-sided accusations. Truth be told, the healthiest approach is to deal directly with the individual who is the source of your frustration.

Most relationship challenges spiral from poor communication and irresponsible to immature misunderstandings. This happens because most people are horrible at communicating their feelings and refuse to seek professional help. Some people are just lazy communicators. Social media, digital lifestyles, and cellular texting have perpetuated poor communication practices. Pity parties and poor communication happens in all types of relationships, not just amongst couples, family, and friends. You might have a higher education than others, a different ethnic background, and a superior philosophy. However, whether male or female, rich or poor, sick or healthy, disabled or advanced, we are all equal as human beings. Respect is the common denominator that allows us to empathize and feel this sense of equality. Without respect, poor communication and emotionally charged misunderstandings thrive. Respect is one of the greatest seeds to improve your harvest of social and emotional wellness.

Respect always honor resolution, even absent of agreement. Relationship issues between couples, family, friends, and others are difficult because personalities are meshed together with different values. People have different experiences that generate an array of opinions causing uncommon criticism and cultural clashing. Unfortunately, in this type of social climate, people who fail to love themselves experience misery, defeat, and anxiety. Just because you say you love yourself doesn't mean that you do. Do you fall to pieces when family and friends don't extend the kind of interaction you think they should? Creating guidelines and stipulations for other people is not love. What happens when other people don't meet your expectations? Instead of going negative, empower yourself for continued improvement. Harboring unhealthy energy and negative thoughts about other people is counterproductive to love. Respect where other people are in life, emotionally, socially and intellectually.

Without this self-preserving love, broken hearted individuals will assimilate to popular opinion, subject themselves to aggressive personalities, and/or have difficulties coping with rejection. Learn to "love yourself first" and avoid this unwanted cycle of emotional deterioration. Love is not controlling. People will try to control you based on your skin complexion, hairstyle, mistakes, weaknesses, and so on. Don't allow it. When you love yourself first, what other people say about you will have no effect. I'll say it again, your journey to improve starts with embracing the reality that you have nothing to prove to others. Afterward, loving yourself will enable you to paint a new and improved mental image.

I've made some serious mistakes in life. I've been the subject of lies and gossip, but none of these experiences define me. Instead, this is how I view myself. I am a kindhearted and caring human being with dignity. I am handsome and I see beauty in others. I put energy into keeping my thoughts and conversations positive and honest. I am confident, in spite of my flaws and failures. I like being alone and I never feel lonely. I enjoy reading, writing, swimming, skating, running, walking, and cooking, things I can do by myself. I'm seldom bored and I feel like there are not enough hours in a day. I am very careful not to think more highly of myself than I ought. I "own" my euphoric state of happiness. I reject anything and/or anybody that attempts to vandalize the portrait of my self-image. My self-esteem comes from embracing the mentality that despite my imperfections and desire to consistently improve, I have nothing to prove to others. When I learned to love myself first, I took possession of everything I needed to be my own best friend. Everybody and everything else is subsequent to the personal priorities that define my identity.

You are who you are. Despite failures, loneliness, and betrayals, I strongly recommend making the ultimate decision to love yourself unconditionally. Make your personal wellness a priority. This is the most successful strategy to strengthen self-esteem. Nothing is greater than love – in the end, love wins.

Chapter **5**

UNDERSTANDING WHAT MATTERS IN THE END

The Seven Dimensions of Wellness

What matters in the end is that you make yourself your own priority. Some people think this concept is selfish, but not so. I used to be one of those people too, but I expanded the horizon of my thinking. For instance, I can't wake my 11-year-old daughter up for school, unless I make it a priority to wake up first. I wouldn't have been able to give my neighbor a ride to the automotive shop, if I didn't make it a priority to own a vehicle. An unmotivated obese individual can't physically train a body builder. I know this because that overweight person was me. I think readers get the point, we have to understand what matters in end. Every individual has seven dimensions of wellness. These dimensions are critical to our personal growth and development. Wellness is a life skill overlooked by most. The dimensions of wellness are not to be confused with our seven body systems; digestive, circulatory, skeletal, respiratory, excretory, nervous and endocrine. However, like the systems of the human body works together, the dimensions of wellness also work hand-in-hand. These dimensions include spiritual, physical, social, emotional, intellectual, occupational and environmental. In the end, nothing is more important than your ability to improve your wellness.

SPIRITUAL WELLNESS

When all is said and done, in order to function as healthy individuals, we must focus on our basic human needs. Our first need is spiritual, because the source of our very essence is spirit. This aspect of our identity is often overlooked. When we learn to acknowledge the things we cannot see, our quality of life will rapidly accelerate. We breathe in oxygen and exhale carbon dioxide without ever seeing it. Without drawing air into our lungs we'd die. Things we cannot see are critical to life and death -- such is the case with spiritual needs.

As a young adult, my life nearly took a different cult-like course because of wayward spiritual views. Religious leaders attempted to aggressively pressure me into an arranged marriage. At the time, I barely knew the young lady. I was only 22-years-old, uneducated, financially unstable, and misguided. I had no clue about spiritual principals. I was publically rebuked, ridiculed, excommunicated and shamed for disobeying the message. This experience nearly damaged my faith. I escaped the snare – not without the pain of broken relationships, unanswered questions, relocating, and experiencing confusion. I can empathize with people who've endured the difficulties of breaking away from religious cults. It's not as easy as it may seem. Spirituality has a significant impact on the human mind. Now, I know the difference between strange nonsense disguised as spirituality vs. a balanced sense of spiritual wellness.

When we ignore our need to exercise faith, embody silence, and embrace beliefs, we neglect our spiritual needs. It's okay to explore, experience, and evaluate different beliefs. In essence, spirituality is the ability to establish peace and harmony in life. Spirituality is the ability to develop a balance between values and actions. It is realizing the common purpose that binds creation together. It's common for people to exalt, empower, and esteem religious leaders, giving them all power over all things spiritual. Be mindful that absolute power corrupts absolutely. We must always remember that no one has a monopoly on spirituality.

PHYSICAL WELLNESS

We are body, soul, and spirit. As a result, our second dimension is physical wellness. In 2017, my family decided to start eating a strict healthy vegan diet. We started focusing on getting an adequate supply of sleep. We increased our water consumption tremendously. As a result, we lost weight and inches. While I'm proud of my results, having lost over 70 pounds, physical health is an ongoing endeavor. I started taking vitamins, exercising, reading healthy lifestyle articles, and searching the ingredients on food packaging labels. I made physical wellness one of my 7 greatest priorities.

Physical wellness is the ability to maintain a healthy quality life without undue fatigue or physical stress. It is the ability to recognize that our behaviors have a significant impact on our wellness. It is also important to adopt healthful habits like routine checkups, a balanced diet, exercise, etc. This also includes avoiding destructive habits like inhaling tobacco, misuse of drugs, excessive alcohol consumption, etc. Also, optimal physical wellness includes avoiding silent killers like stress.

Stress can potentially lead to serious sickness. This is why I strongly encourage readers to avoid people, places and things that create unhealthy hassles. I place emphasis on unhealthy stress, because stress is impossible to avoid. It's important to know the difference between different types of stress. Some stress can be controlled, such as stress induced by exercise or employment. This type of stress is key for survival. However, too much stress can be detrimental. Specifically, long term emotional stress weakens the immune system, causes high blood pressure, anxiety, and even heart disease. Consult a physician for more information concerning unhealthy amounts of stress, especially if you worry a lot. You have the ultimate responsibility to take care of yourself physically.

All too often people blame others for their own self-created problems. You alone have the final say so of how to deal with anything that happens in your life. As social beings, we have needs. Socially, our lives have the potential of rapidly going from uncomplicatedness to unrest. It's important to understand how to escape toxic relationships that will only ruin your efforts to improve your life.

SOCIAL WELLNESS

Human wellness has a lot to do with a healthy social life. Recent studies have shown that healthy social relationships can save your life, literally. Active social lives have been shown to reduce a person's risk of early death by 50 percent. As a result of healthy social connections, there have been more than 5 people who have made their children my namesakes. On the other hand, connecting with conniving, hurting, miserable, unhappy people defies peace and promotes chaos. Beware of pretenders, people hiding their pain behind happy faces. Yes, there are individuals who pretend to be happy. In fact, pretending to be happy and drama-free is currently trending. It's ironic, because the people who spew negative spectacles, are the first to reply, "I don't like drama". Socially messy individuals claim to despise mess. As a result, these people seldom find true happiness. They stay stuck sucking others into their disastrous hurricane of gossip, negativity, and manipulation.

When we connect socially, we naturally share a piece of our identity. Unknowingly, social connections cause us to embrace certain character traits from friends and family. This happens unintentionally, whether we want it to or not. We put ourselves in jeopardy when we connect and commit to new friendships without a thorough assessment. Listen to people and watch their action, this will show you who they really are. Afterward, when people show you who they are, believe them. Most importantly, weigh people's perspectives about life and love. Lifelong friendships are not waged overnight. Stop expecting something for nothing. In such scenarios, you'll end up dealing with difficult dilemmas scripted by individuals who do not have your best interest.

Make wiser choices about the people you allow in your life. As for family and close friends, do not tolerate shenanigans. If you feel like you are socially in bondage, herein lies a problem that you must deal with. Social well-being is critical to personal identity. Don't allow people to bully you into dealing with superficially-created-drama. Relationship titles don't give people the authority to serve as Lord over your life. Don't allow loved-ones to control your social life with threatening ultimatums. Much like your spiritual and physical health, you alone are responsible for your social well-being. Do not allow anyone to control your personal relationships.

I've seen spouses socially reject their extended family, only to get divorced and crawl back crying. I've seen in-laws mistreat one another based on unnecessary opinions. Don't entertain these dysfunctional social concepts – boldly ignore them. I've seen people put in awkward positions between opposing individuals, forced to take sides, and then betrayed by the so-called friend they supported. Social wellness is most complicated, but physical wellness is more difficult. That's because wellness is far more meaningful than scrolling through social media clicking "like". People poorly communicate about important subjects by sending distorted texts with the latest emoji. Social wellness requires a concerted effort to dialog in detail. Any other effort derails relationships. Social wellness is not fortified by passive comments. It is not stimulated by social media posts. Ultimately, social wellness demands engaged conversation void of constant distractions. In fact, I'd argue that social media is creating a disengaged-self-centered culture with hideous habits that destroy relationships. Most people are keenly aware that social media is an unhealthy social distraction. It's a platform, and sometimes even a bully pulpit, that gives voice to the unlearned, inexperienced, and disengaged. While people prowl and lurk behind their computer screens and cellular devices, businesses actually benefit with advertisement. Social media isn't going anywhere anytime soon, but if you ever expect to achieve social wellness, know that social media will hinder your efforts. Social wellness is the ability to relate to and connect with other people in our world.

EMOTIONAL WELLNESS

Emotional wellness is the ability to understand ourselves and cope with life's most challenging changes. The ability to acknowledge and/or share feelings of anger, fear, sadness or stress; hope, love, joy and happiness in a productive manner contributes to our emotional wellness.

Everybody has the right to feel however he or she feels. Allow no one to manipulate you into guilt because of how you feel. On the other hand, maturity has a lot to do with how we allow our feelings to transition into emotions. Feelings do not fuel dysfunctional. How we act on our feelings is what causes reactions.

I've seen a mother discontinue her relationship with an adult daughter because of anger. I've experience the suicidal loss of a friend because of mismanaged feelings. I've seen couples get divorced because of their inability to communicate feelings verbally and nonverbally. At the end of the day, emotionally well individuals possess the maturity and strength to redirect their feelings.

Emotional wellness is learning to understand ourselves and cope with changes and challenges, not control others and lash out at unwanted circumstances. Emotions are a glaring give-a-away to measure maturity. Emotional wellness effects our ability to avoid depression, post-partum, insanity, and other psychological disorders. America is inundated with emotional dysfunction, because people are seldom taught the significance of emotional wellness.

ENVIRONMENTAL WELLNESS

Environment, occupational and intellectual wellness are our final three dimensions to transition to a quality life. Environmental wellness is the ability to be responsible for the quality of the air, water and the land. Environmental wellness is our ability to make a positive impact on the quality of our planet.

OCCUPATIONAL WELLNESS

Have you ever met someone who hated their job? Even worse, I have friends and associates with college degrees that consistently complain about their employment. The problem is they do nothing to change it. They have the education and wherewithal to produce expected outcomes, but they find a sense of contentment complaining rather than changing. I realize change is not easy. In 2017, an additional 1.7 million new jobs were created in America. Entrepreneurial opportunities are soaring. Occupational wellness is the ability to get personal fulfillment from the work that we do.

Feeling a sense of purpose from the work we do is imperative. However, don't become so engulfed in your work that you fail to make family and friends a priority. Occupational wellness is gaining a self of career-worth while still maintaining a work/life balanced. Occupational wellness is contributing in our careers, making a positive impact in society, and sustaining a solid sense of respect in your personal life outside of work. This is not always easy to do, but chip away at it daily. Make goals. Occupational wellness is an important reality in each of our lives. Occupational wellness sometimes requires additional training, more education, and career counseling. Without this dimension of wellness, the other six dimensions will possess little worth. It's like exercising while eating unhealthy, or telling the truth while living a lie. These dimensions of wellness are directly connected to living an overall quality life.

INTELLECTUAL WELLNESS

Lastly, intellectual wellness is the ability to open your mind to new ideas. As productive individuals, we intellectually engage in experiences that enrich communities. As we personally improve our lives, it will inevitably reflect in the betterment of our communities. Intellectual wellness is acting on the desire to learn new concepts, improve skills and seek challenges.

Intellectual wellness should not clash with, or contradict occupational wellness. When I engage in new ideas, I aim to keep my focus centered on multimedia/journalism. I've organized benefit concerts, hosted book signing, marketed schools, and volunteered on international mission trips. Every endeavor always engages my journalistic expertise.

Intellectual wellness is a pursuit of lifelong learning. Understanding what matters in the end keeps us focused on properly pursuing the life objective of happiness. Remember, I am not a psychologist, therapist or licensed counselor. This book contains a culmination of real life experiences and introspections intended to help readers glean from shared ideas. Oprah Winfrey once said, "Speaking your truth is the most powerful tool we all have." This book is my truth. I hope it empowers individuals with the tools needed to improve reader's lives one step at a time.

In the end, wellness matters in every area of your life. Use this short book as a guide to get started with improvements. You alone are responsible for your personal wellness and individual happiness. When you first get started, discipline will be in high demand. Soon after, improving your life will simply become a habit. Greek philosopher Aristotle said, "What we repeatedly do is what we become, excellence is not an act, it is a habit." Create the kind of habits that will cause your short life to improve.